DEEP IN MY FEELS

Also by Jennae Cecelia

come be cozy

don't hurry to tomorrow

meet me at golden hour

healing for no one but me

the sun will rise and so will we

the moon will shine for us too

losing myself brought me here

dear me at fifteen

i am more than my nightmares

uncaged wallflower—extended edition

i am more than a daydream

uncaged wallflower

bright minds empty souls

DEEP IN MY FEELS

JENNAE CECELIA

Andrews McMeel
PUBLISHING®

Deep in My Feels copyright © 2025 by Jennae Cecelia All rights reserved. Printed in China. No part of this book may be used or reproduced in any manner whatsoever without written permission, except in the case of reprints in the context of reviews.

Andrews McMeel Publishing
a division of Andrews McMeel Universal
1130 Walnut Street, Kansas City, Missouri 64106

www.andrewsmcmeel.com

25 26 27 28 29 TEN 10 9 8 7 6 5 4 3 2 1

ISBN: 979-8-8816-0030-3

Library of Congress Control Number: 2025930307

Editor: Danys Mares
Art Director/Designer: Tiffany Meairs
Production Editor: David Shaw
Production Manager: Julie Skalla

ATTENTION: SCHOOLS AND BUSINESSES

Andrews McMeel books are available at quantity discounts with bulk purchase for educational, business, or sales promotional use. For information, please email the Andrews McMeel Publishing Special Sales Department: sales@andrewsmcmeel.com.

when vulnerability is hard, *deep in my feels* is here
to remind you that sharing your feelings
is not only okay but necessary.

for my husband—
the guy who sat next to me in class all those years ago
and told me to make sure i write the book.
well, here we are.
my biggest supporter, my best friend, and my love.

dear reader,

writing poetry is my therapy. i look at it as a way to convey emotions that others can relate to but don't know how to articulate themselves. and what a blessing it is to be able to do that.

i have always been the type of person to feel things very deeply. often told by others that i think too deep and go too deep. but i have never been the type to want to hang out in the shallow end.

when writing *deep in my feels*, i wanted to share words with you that would inspire you to open up about your losses and vulnerable moments. to write them down or tell a trusted friend. to no longer feel the need to keep your emotions locked inside. i wanted to invite you to open up and let it all out. cry. know that you are not alone in the feelings you experience throughout this life.

now, let's get deep.

Love,
Jennae

CONTENTS

LOVING DEEPLY.........1

GETTING VULNERABLE.........65

FEELING HOPEFUL...............119

LOVING DEEPLY

i'm waiting for a man who is nurturing and intentional.
i'll stay boy sober as long as it takes.
i know they say the men in the books
aren't like that in real life,
but why can't they be?
why does it have to be considered a reach
to think that someone could treat you with empathy and respect?
i don't want to be alone forever,
but i also don't want to be with someone just to say
i achieved what society is hoping from me.

DEEP IN MY FEELS

it's autumn.
the leaves are turning
shades of orange and yellow.
i wear your sweatshirt
with your college's name.
but things don't feel the same.

you're far away.
and you barely call.
i see online that you have
gone to every party this year.
a few girls tagged you in photos
and i pretend not to care.

but i am up all night thinking about
what you are doing
and who you are seeing.
wondering if you even think about me.
it has been only two months since you left.
but the leaves are turning colors,

and i am wondering if we
are going to fall with them.

Jennae Cecelia

i laugh at all of your jokes
even when they aren't that funny.

we always go to the restaurants that you like
even if nothing on the menu sounds appealing
to me.

i talk quieter when you want to be louder
even though my mind is eager to have a turn.

you will say that you are blindsided.
when i tell you i am unhappy and finally leave.

because you thought everything was okay.
and i will feel like it is my fault again
for not making my needs noticed.

but if i have to beg to have things
even slightly my way,
well, we were bound to crash and burn
at the end of the day.

i clung to the friends we shared
in hopes of hearing about you in between sips of drinks.
how you were doing or if you ever mentioned me.
i know you ended things,
but i didn't think we would never speak again.
what happened to
we can still be friends?

Jennae Cecelia

i have always felt like the friend in the group
who can easily be replaced.
that no one would question
why i didn't make it to an event that day.
my presence wasn't missed.
and even when i did show up,
i was a fly on a wall without even knowing it.

DEEP IN MY FEELS

your dad called.
it has been over a year.
i'm protective of your heart
so i say you aren't here.
he says under his breath
about you ignoring him.
but i know the chances of that are slim.
it is he who has been ignoring you.
and now that he wants to show up,
he is mad that you don't too.
but i let him know you are worth so much more
than a call here and there.
you are the person who
spreads light everywhere.
and i don't want him dimming
what you have worked so hard to make shine.
he doesn't just get to decide when he wants to
be a part of your life.

i thought the world would come crashing down around me
when you closed the door between you and me.
but instead,
it opened windows that let fresh air in,
and i feel like i can finally breathe again.

DEEP IN MY FEELS

when you yell at me for the first time,
i try to tell myself that
beautiful boys can't be mean.

and when you ignore me and call me names,
i try to tell myself that
beautiful boys can't be cruel.

i will make up excuses for you.
tie them together with a pretty bow.
because beautiful boys are shiny and new.

but some of them have an ugliness
that i wish i never knew.

i'll never forget the friend i had in sixth grade
buying me clothes for my birthday
that she knew wouldn't fit.
XXS
not even close to the size i was then.
and then she would proceed to say,
try it on for us.
we want to see.
i quickly learned that
she wasn't my best friend.
she was my enemy.

DEEP IN MY FEELS

remember this:
it's the nice guy who will love your children well.
wipe their tears instead of telling them not to cry.
endless patience as they learn to ride a bike.
listen before getting upset that they came home late at night.
at the end of the day,
it's the nice guy.

we stared at the blue sky together.
at the clouds as they rolled in.
i told you secrets
that i couldn't tell my family or friends.
because they had judgment and opinions,
and you just listened.

DEEP IN MY FEELS

i was lost from your life
but quickly replaced.
so i guess i wasn't as special
as you made me seem.
was i even important to you
or were you just pretending?
were the *i love you*s fake?
were the late-night conversations just lies?
you are still all i think about,
and yet somehow you moved on in no time.

she is sunday brunch with your family.
i am a last-minute granola bar
on your way out the door.
always an afterthought.
never more.

DEEP IN MY FEELS

you seem more put together than the rest.
i let out a small breath
as i listened to him.
i get that a lot.
that i am too put together
to be caught up with someone like you.
but something about me thinks
i can always be the one to fix what needs fixing.
even though that will never be true.

Jennae Cecelia

i was always a glass-half-full kind of person.
until you kept pouring out what i had left
over and over again.
and somewhere along the way
i started to believe
that all there was to see
was emptiness.
you took optimism from me.

i would make you a birthday cake from scratch.
you would forget my birthday.
i always loved you more.

i was constantly bouncing between
sadness and happiness with you.
our morning filled with fun
ruined by a silly argument in the afternoon.
i asked to see your phone
and you hesitated a bit.
the same phone that hours before was
taking photos of us laughing as the sun rolled in.
tomorrow we will repeat the same cycle over again.

i don't know why i questioned if we should be together
because i didn't even want to be your friend.

DEEP IN MY FEELS

you told me that your favorite song
was taylor swift's "red."
that you liked art fairs
and poetry readings
and that you also had dreams of starting a homestead.
but i think you said this because
you were trying to get inside my head
and in my bed.
anything but be real with me.
just saying what would leave me pleased.
even if it meant losing your authenticity.

i was done turning my world around for him.
the plans i made needing to fit his.
sacrificing what i wanted.
i was the last to get,
always the first to give.

DEEP IN MY FEELS

when i see you out years from now
with your new girlfriend
or maybe even your wife,
you can pretend like we never met.
that's fine.

i will go along with it.
you can call us old friends.
maybe even just colleagues.
that's fine.

because deep down we both know
how much we mattered to each other
all those years ago.

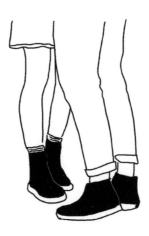

i bet your dog misses me.
i bet he whines in the bay window
where i used to read for hours with him as he slept content.
i bet he is longing for me to come back.
i bet he is wondering where i am.
i bet he curls up on the side of the bed i slept on
that is still holding on to hints of my warm vanilla perfume.
i bet he brings you the fleetwood mac t-shirt of yours that i always wore.
i bet you tell him i left him behind.
i bet you hate that he keeps reminding you
i once existed in your space.

i thought i loved you.
i thought i knew
what those words really meant.
but i only said i love you because
i thought i was supposed to.
really,
i just feel emptiness.

Jennae Cecelia

facebook memories remind me you existed.
though it's not like i could forget
the love we shared back then.
it shows us laughing in the back seat
of your best friend's car.
dancing together at an old run-down bar.
i wonder if these are the first things
that pop up when you open your facebook page.
i doubt you see,
because i noticed
you haven't posted anything since 2019.

DEEP IN MY FEELS

i was holding the most beautiful person in my hands.
and i let them slip away.
because it was hard to be with someone
who could love me well.
i was too used to self-sabotage and pain.

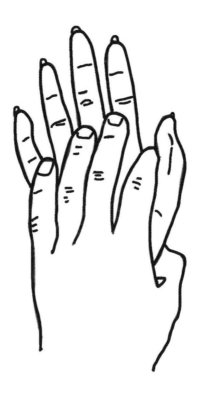

Jennae Cecelia

they weren't really in love.
because *in love* doesn't look like
doing exactly what they want you to do
out of fear that it will start an argument.

in love doesn't look like being okay
with everything they say
but in your head
you have complaints.

in love shouldn't be turning yourself
into a person who fully pleases the other
while sacrificing who you are.

they weren't really in love.
it was for show.
and oh what a show they put on.

DEEP IN MY FEELS

the loss of a friendship
hits deeper than any relationship
i have ever been in.
the girlhood we once shared
were peak times,
i swear.
stayed up late
to watch the hannah montana premiere.
snuck into the stash of chocolate chip cookies
your mom baked.
recorded music videos
for only us to watch back and laugh at.
now it feels like i am supposed to pretend
like it didn't even happen.
that i wasn't the one who
stayed up late with you on the phone
when your high school boyfriend kissed another girl.
hugged you as you cried after your mom called you fat
for not fitting into the same dress she wore at your age.
held your hair while sitting on the cold bathroom floor
the first time that you drank.
distant memories are all they are now.
but one day i hope to get the courage to tell you
i miss you and the memories we made.

i learned quickly that it was never about me
or my wants and needs.
it was only what you wanted.
and you found someone like me,
who would give in so easily.
the perfect person for you.
because i did everything you wanted me to.

the time you wanted to take to
discover yourself
ended fast.
you are already with someone new.
which makes me think
she was the one you were interested in
discovering all along.

if ghosts are real,
why don't you haunt me?
make yourself known.
follow me around
when i feel alone.
send me little signs that you are near.
if ghosts are real,
why don't you let me know you are here?

DEEP IN MY FEELS

i was the gossip over dinner.
shared like an appetizer between friends.
i wasn't there,
so i can't confirm it,
but i heard that you think i am annoying and needy.
which is interesting because you were always the one
who told me i could confide in you with my secrets and fears.
was it with good intention?
because i am starting to think
you secretly like to see me in tears.

i would say i am a little jealous
of who you get to be.
because i am nowhere near the place
i want to be.
and you have become
everything you have hoped to be.
and let's be honest,
you wouldn't be in this place without me.

DEEP IN MY FEELS

your new girlfriend
has looked me up on social media.
i can see her watching my stories.
at first i was annoyed,
but then i wondered if there is a reason
she is watching me.

is she silently wondering
what life after you looks like?
no fights.
no yelling.
no being talked down to all day and night.

tonight, instead of being annoyed,
i say a silent prayer
that she learns who you really are
quickly.

DEEP IN MY FEELS

what i would do to have
someone real by my side.
a true love in this life.
not a person who comes and goes.
never meeting their family
or seeing their childhood home.
who i thought they would be in my life
is no longer the picture that is painted.
here i am again with a blank canvas
and a heart that is tainted.

when i miss you,
i reread our conversations
until i fall asleep.
wishing i could change things.
are you missing me?

all i have are the words already said,
the butterflies i wish to feel again,
and the short goodnight text i hoped you'd send.
to know moments with me appeared in your mind
right before bed.

DEEP IN MY FEELS

i wasn't the best friend.
i was just your friend.
even though i did best friend things.
cleaned your house when you were sick.
walked your dog when you were late getting in.
but you didn't do the same for me.

instead, you text me a few days after my birthday
and say time just got away.
you show up with dessert covered in nuts
and say you forgot i was allergic to them.
just scrape them off. it will be okay.

i was always present for you,
but for me you were never here.
i was always misreading what we were,
even though in the details you made it clear.

we are fading summer.
the pinks and blues
bleeding together.
the sunscreen replaced
with a knit sweater.
the final goodnight is lingering in the air.
our summer is fading,
and i am not ready to tell you goodbye.

DEEP IN MY FEELS

i wore your favorite color
more than my own.
anything to make you love me
a little bit more.
but i am sure my effort
will be ignored.

you said you didn't know i was anxious.

but didn't you see my dilated pupils?
my knee bouncing up and down.
the way i bite the side of my nails.
the clearing of my throat.

did you just ignore all of the signs
that i was not fine?
was it too much of a bother
for you to ask me?
or did you just not want to know?

DEEP IN MY FEELS

i'll quickly apologize
and retract any statement
that comes out of my mouth
when i notice you hesitate to answer
and your face goes blank.
i worry you aren't going to like
whatever i may say.
i need reassurance about everything.

do you understand that i don't want to be
with anyone who doesn't light up my life
like the stars do the night sky?
i want the sun in my life.
the full moon bright.
i don't want to settle for candlelight.

DEEP IN MY FEELS

it was late august.
you wanted me to leave
but you didn't want to say it,
so you just stopped answering me.

the texts and calls became less.
i would wait around holding my breath.

the eagerness of june had faded.
and the fire we ignited in july had no flame.
a summer fling is all it was to you.

and here i was naively thinking
this was a love we would see through.

Jennae Cecelia

i'll hide out in little coffee shops
and indie bookstores
because they are things i love
and i know i won't see you there.
you always made it clear
that what i loved was silly and boring.
so i go to the places i know
i will never hear a barista call out your name.

DEEP IN MY FEELS

the door was closed and felt permanent.
but *hellos* can happen again.

one day there was a faint knock.
just a hint.
and even though you said you wouldn't,
you got curious.

you say you will only open the door
just a crack.
two inches to be exact.

except deep down
you know that isn't true.
because once you allow them in
even just a bit,
it is game over for you.

we talked about
what we would do for our birthdays.
the hotel we would book
with the money we didn't have.

the reservations we would make
at the five-star restaurant
where the servers wear
white gloves on their hands.

the bottle of champagne we would pop
that was really only a few dollars at the corner store.
but we never made it to our birthdays.
so it is just me alone on my bedroom floor.

the take-out restaurant gave me
enough plasticware for two.
and silently i hum to myself,
happy birthday to you.

maybe in another life
we cross paths again.
waiting in line for coffee.
in a crowd at a concert.
at a new restaurant in town.
and the years we missed won't matter.
because here we are now.

you tell him that i am not good enough,
and i will cry to you the next day
when he breaks it off.
little did i know it was because of you.
the girl who said she was my number one fan.
but really to her my life falling apart
was just good entertainment.

DEEP IN MY FEELS

i wish i could forget
as easily as he did.
but nostalgia and romance
run in my veins.

wide eyed at your door.
you told me you didn't want me anymore.

your mother was in the kitchen
making family dinner.
her smile felt like home as she approached us.
she didn't know you'd just ended things.

on the verge of breaking down
you tried to get me to leave in a rush.
out to the car and away from here.
before anyone could see my tears.

and i didn't just lose you that day.
i lost the family too.

i wonder if your mom still asks about me over dinner.
i wonder if she knows that it ended because of you.

DEEP IN MY FEELS

alone tonight
i pour two glasses of wine.
one for you.
one for me.
sit at the table where we used to laugh and fight.
this is the funeral for us
and who we could have been together.
the bottle is finished
and we aren't getting another.

they will tell me
he was ugly anyway.
but i know that isn't true.
he was the most beautiful person i had ever met.
he just wasn't ready to fall in love yet,
i will tell myself.
while holding my breath
waiting for him to come back.
but for now,
i nod slightly in agreement
when my friends say he was ugly anyway.

DEEP IN MY FEELS

i liked you better before there was her.
your genuine smile has begun to fade.
now you eat dinner after you pray.
her dad took you golfing, and i chuckle a bit
because i know you hated every second of it.
your band t-shirts replaced with polos that button up.
you look uncomfortable,
but this is what you were told is love.
sacrificing who you want to be
just to fit in with high society.

morning comes and still my phone is blank.
besides a text letting me know
i have a dentist appointment next week.

my heart sinks.
but it shouldn't.
this isn't anything new.

i wait around forever and you probably have yet
to think about what i am up to.

DEEP IN MY FEELS

i think i don't miss you,
but as i bake in the kitchen,
i think of how you would be here
asking to lick the whisk.
i would laugh as the batter drips down your chin.
it's in those small moments,
when there is this unexplained emptiness,
that you're truly missed.

DEEP IN MY FEELS

you told me you didn't want to kiss me too soon.
we just crossed the bridge from friends to more.
this was a day i had waited for.
you no longer seeing
my freckles on my neck as childish marks.
you were eager for your lips to meet the places
you have only watched from a distance
but longed to find in the dark.
closing the gap between friends
and something more.
everything we have waited for.

Jennae Cecelia

in the daylight
i would say i don't miss you.
that i never even think of you.
that my day is too busy and
my mind has no time to hit rewind on our memories.

but at night
flashbacks of you by my side are on repeat.
i can't sleep because the space beside me is now empty.

the world is silent and so is this room
that once was filled with
so much love and laughter with you.

DEEP IN MY FEELS

i didn't think anything of it at first
when you started to come home late.
on your phone as i put the now cold dinner on your plate.
only half listening to me tell you about my day,
and yet you have the audacity to complain.

i can see the smile on your face.
as you reach quickly to reply to the message on your phone.
you get up abruptly from the table to shower.
and i know it's another night being alone.

i didn't think anything of it at first,
because i didn't want to admit
it was over long before i had the chance to save it.

right person,
wrong time.
the distance between us has grown.
your name in my call log
has slowly drifted to the bottom.
our anniversary passed
and any hope of you reaching out
left with it.
you said you know we were meant to be,
just not at this time.
maybe in a few years
when we experienced more life.
but i won't wait forever for you.
not that you are asking me to.
i bet you already found someone new.
right person,
right time
for you.

DEEP IN MY FEELS

i'm scared to fall in love.
do the benefits outweigh the risk?
handing my heart to someone
and holding my breath.
wondering if it is safe in their hands
or if they will be careless with it.

i'm scared to fall in love
and i feel like no one truly understands.
they are willing to take the risk.
fall in love over and over again.
but i know i can't handle it.

i get attached too quickly,
and then before i know it,
they are onto someone new.

Jennae Cecelia

the first time you told me to shut up
i was so taken aback that i think i laughed.
until i realized you didn't crack a smile.
that you really meant it.
i watched your face go red.
i quietly apologized and you just stood right there
looking at me intensely.
that day you went from being the person i thought i could love
to the person i would do anything to forget.

DEEP IN MY FEELS

there is a lot to unpack.
where do i begin?
i don't want to trauma dump on you.
but it is hard not to.
when i have bottled up feelings for so long,
it all starts to spill out fast.
the moments that i have hid in the past.
scars healed with time,
but only time.
not because they were ever addressed.
i never got the stitches i truly needed.
i just hoped for the best.

DEEP IN MY FEELS

i have let my hair get greasier than normal.
it hurts to brush through.

it's only tuesday,
but it feels like it should be friday.
the makeup under my eyes is smeared.
i have cried endless tears.

i forgot how to get dressed
in anything other than sweatpants.
even just brushing my teeth
is exhausting.

they call it the pit.
but i think i fell deep.
i don't know the last time
the sun and i met.

i was afraid of letting go of friendships
that no longer served me
because everyone else had these lifelong friends.
and how embarrassing that i couldn't ever find them.
that i didn't have a best friend from the first grade
who grew up to be each other's bridesmaids.
i mourn that i lack the nostalgia of girlhood
that bleeds into womanhood.
where we can reminisce on
our seasons of life together that run so deep,
while our kids we once talked about as little girls
now run barefoot in the street.
i think i will forever miss
that i never got that type of friendship.

DEEP IN MY FEELS

i can still feel your breath on my neck.
and not in a good way.
you are everywhere i turn
and i don't want you to be.

you tell me if what i am wearing
is okay enough for you.
i can't remember the last time
i was alone with my own thoughts
without them being interrupted and guided
on which way to go.

who am i without you?
some days i feel like i will never know.

Jennae Cecelia

i bump into a stranger at the grocery store
and i'm not able to get out the words
i'm sorry.
instead, i mumble and frantically walk away.
they probably think i'm rude.

i will forget half the food on my list
because i am too busy thinking over and over again
about how i bumped into them.
i replay it in my mind.
apologize more boldly this time.

i will drive home and not notice the songs on the radio
because i am too busy thinking about what that person
must think of me now.
are they telling their friends about the rude encounter
they had?
worse, did they post it on social media to vent?
will it go viral and people will question who i am?

why is my mind like this?

DEEP IN MY FEELS

it's may.
the sun is up a little longer.
the flowers are starting to fully bloom.
i wear my favorite t-shirt and jeans.
but worry about having to show my legs soon.
why does this happen every may?
things are beautiful,
but i don't feel the same.

i hated the smell of cigarettes,
but here we are on the back porch
and you put one in my hand.
i couldn't stand the taste of beer,
but here i am sipping it along with you.
all the things i was told i shouldn't do.
but i was trying to feel something.
anything really.
because no one cared about me
when i was quietly listening.
so why not make some noise?

DEEP IN MY FEELS

i saw a girl i went to high school with at the mall.
she didn't recognize me at all.
even though we were lab partners
for two semesters.
was it the years between then and now
or was i still just as invisible
as i was back then?
couldn't be her friend.
even get a hi.
nothing has changed except time.
but i try not to judge her.
maybe she truly doesn't remember me.
because honestly
i don't even remember
who i used to be.

Jennae Cecelia

i realized somewhere along the way
i stopped getting excited for summer.
or any season change.
it all started to feel the same.
beautiful to others.
full of prosperity.
but i was so deep
in the feelings surrounding me
that getting excited was even more exhausting.

DEEP IN MY FEELS

i feel guilty when my anxiety takes over
and the girl who used to be
on top of everything falls.

the girl who remembered
everyone's favorite color
can barely remember her own.

the girl who would
make sure to text and check in
and ask if you need anything
can now barely look at her phone
without dread.
my anxiety takes over
and i don't even know how to
leave my bed.

and i know that you who have
never faced anxiety will say
it isn't that hard to just
pull yourself together.
i wish it was that easy.

but for me that is going outside
without an umbrella
in downpour rainy weather.

and then one day i will feel better.
for really no reason at all.
i'll pick up the phone again
eager to call.
make plans.
be a helping hand
to those in need.

god i would never complain
if it meant not getting sucked back in by anxiety.

DEEP IN MY FEELS

are you snacking because you are hungry
or are you bored?
that is when it all started.
when i was told my intuition wasn't right.
that there was no way i could be hungry already.
that i needed to eat a bigger lunch.
not eat breakfast in a rush.
not stay up late and watch tv
with a bowl of chips.
i didn't know how to be in tune with my own body
because someone else was in control of the pitch.

sisterhood of the traveling pants made me feel like
i wouldn't have to worry about sharing clothes
with friends who didn't match my size.
they could all exchange clothes,
but why couldn't i?
i had already started recognizing at a young age
that my body and their bodies didn't look the same.
and i don't think i have ever fully loved myself since that day.

DEEP IN MY FEELS

you will say i kept secrets from you,
but i want you to know
you were the one who didn't create a space
for me to come to you.

there were food and drinks
after your funeral.
people lined up to get their plate.
i heard a few people talk about
how dry their sandwiches were.
how could they complain?
how could they even eat?
did we not all just go through
one of the worst days of our lives?
or was that just me?
everyone else is smiling and even laughing while they
converse in their black outfits
and smell of cheap perfume.
all i want is to scream and leave the room.
except as i try to leave, an aunt i haven't seen in years
stops to ask me how i have been.
how have i been?
are we not at the same solemn event?
life just keeps moving, doesn't it?
so quickly it feels like people forget.

DEEP IN MY FEELS

it was better than a therapy session.
the way i met the stars at night.
the way the sunrise was where i felt most at peace.
the silent moments when it seemed
like everyone else was asleep.
and i would let out a scream.

everything i could have ever hoped for is coming true,
so why do i not feel as excited as i thought i would?
is it because i am afraid that all of this good
must mean that bad is on the way?
that i should count my final good days
before it all comes crashing down
just like i told myself it would?
i can't get excited because it scares me.
i fear my excitement is on borrowed time.

DEEP IN MY FEELS

i am fragile,
but somehow it is hard to break me.
your words cut me deep.
but i won't let you see me bleed.
i'll put on a straight face
and pretend to be alright.
when i am alone,
the dam i have built all day will break.

i was told my fragility is only for me to see.
now everyone else thinks
i am stone cold and mean.

i feel like i am forging my whole life.
writing a plot that doesn't truly fit mine.
pretending to be something that i am not.
i smile when i don't mean it.
i laugh when i find nothing funny.

playing pretend has always been
something i am good at.

DEEP IN MY FEELS

out at sea.
waist deep.
i don't think anyone notices
i am drowning.
i am still smiling.
i am laughing as i go.
silently slipping under
and nobody knows.

i think that everyone is staring at me.
noticing all the flaws that i see.
laughing at me.
whispering in each other's ears
when i can't see.
making fun of me.
i tell myself everyone hates me
before i even give them a chance
to show me they don't.
i overthink everything
and i think that they know.

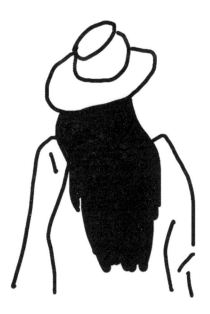

DEEP IN MY FEELS

i never want my child to see me
always avoiding the chips on the table.
having a hot dog with no bun.
repeatedly saying no to dessert.
wondering why i am no fun.
i don't want them thinking
that they also have to live this life.
hating on their body with their own mind.
never enjoying moments
because how they look
becomes more important
than having fun in the moment.

i will question why i am extra anxious
and in such a bad mood.
i will blame it on the new moon
or mercury being in retrograde,
long before i will admit
that it is probably from me
doomscrolling late at night before bed.

it is raining again in my head,
yet for everyone else it is sunny.
why is the bad weather affecting only me?
they are all out
playing,
dancing.
here i am
sad,
alone.
the waters have come and washed me out.
but sadness floods every part of me.
and everyone else seems so happy.

Jennae Cecelia

the wine that met my lips that night
gave me the confidence i needed
to feel like i belonged.
like the walls around me weren't closing in.
that i could be a part of
these small talk conversations.
a boost in my self-esteem
was all i would need.
except it didn't stop at a sip.
it was a whole bottle and some.
why is it to be in these social situations
i need to feel numb?

DEEP IN MY FEELS

there is nothing worse than
treating a wound others can't see.
it's my mind that needs fixing.
there is no blood to show.
no cuts on my knees
or scrapes on my hands.
the pain i have is hidden away.
so they will tell me i am okay.
because really i do look just fine.
but god do i wish they could
just see my mind.

Jennae Cecelia

i notice everything right with her.
i notice everything wrong with me.
my body is not her body.
her body is not mine.
the constant comparison
is what is ruining my life.

DEEP IN MY FEELS

it is a bottle of red wine.
me, myself, and i.
my phone is silent.
no messages to be found.
i sit and stare.
dinner for one tonight.
i say i don't care.
i love being independent.
i don't need someone to feel fulfilled.
but i have no one to share
the big moments with.
to laugh at funny videos i find.
it is another weekend
where i say i am okay being alone,
but sometimes i crave company
besides just me, myself, and i.

i am the sponge absorbing
everyone's pain and worries.
the person they find comfort in.
to let them know they aren't alone.
but when they have gotten what they want,
they wring me out and leave me to dry.
and i am constantly giving so much
while i am being drained of life.

DEEP IN MY FEELS

i wasn't always a lonely girl.
i had a roster of friends.
a village i could call on.
but i changed
and people left.

how are you really?
my friend will ask.
and i let out a sigh and start spilling my life.
i don't know if i have even taken one deep breath this week.
my mind is running in circles and i keep forgetting to eat.
i have danced with procrastination a few too many times.
now i am unhappy with where i am in life.
everyone else seems to have it all together.
they have sunshine and blue skies.
i have downpour weather.
when are things going to get better?

DEEP IN MY FEELS

can i tell you a secret?
hang my laundry out to dry?
i no longer care what people may think.
i want to get deep.
fully expose who i am.
i want to breathe out honesty for the first time.
not have to backtrack
or think of the different plots i have written
to fit who i am talking to.
i want to be fully myself even if that means
making other people uncomfortable with
who they thought me to be.

i wonder if my therapist goes home
and tells her family about me.
narrating my problems
as they pass the potatoes and roast beef.
is her family perfectly put together?
a home-cooked meal and smiles exchanged.
or does her daughter hide things from her,
is her son eager to leave the room?

i wonder if my therapist actually has it all together
or if she is facing her own unnoticed pain.

DEEP IN MY FEELS

i would tell myself
put-together girls don't fall asleep watching tv.

i would tell myself
put-together girls don't avoid conversations.

i would tell myself
put-together girls are easy to love.

i would tell myself
put-together girls look down on you.

i would tell myself
you are not a put-together girl.

Jennae Cecelia

i smell blueberry muffins and bacon
coming from the kitchen.
it's sunday and i thought
i wouldn't make it here.
the past few days have been a blur.
hell, even the past few years.
but my grandma greets me with a plate.
tells me she loves me
and that she is glad that i came.
and now i remember,
it's these moments i hold
when i feel most alone.

DEEP IN MY FEELS

one day i may have a daughter or son.
i will have my arms wide open as they run to me.
i will look them in the eyes and say,
i am so sorry it took me this long to get you here.
and they will smile back at me and say,
what do you mean? i am here at just the right time.

the room they breathed so much life into
is now dull and empty without them.
the recipe they made doesn't taste the same
when you try to repeat it.
the table is set for two,
even though one won't be touched.
the current event they would have been laughing at
is something they will never know.
losing people isn't just them being gone.
it is being reminded of them everywhere you go.

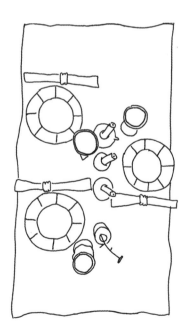

DEEP IN MY FEELS

i am afraid to go to sleep.
not because i don't want to dream.
but because nightmares have taken their place.
cold sweat.
heart race.
the pain in my real life
now blurring into my sleep.
my eyes opened or closed,
it is all a nightmare to me.

my anxiety never allows for me to be fully happy.
i am constantly waiting for a jump scare around the corner.
the other shoe to drop.
the phone to ring with the bad news i dwelled on
and then worry i manifested it.
i have played out horrible scenarios
because my anxiety tells me to.
it is hard to be fully happy when anxiety lives in you.

going to the pool as a kid looked a lot different.
i didn't think about the aesthetics.
i was worried about swimming like a mermaid
and making the biggest splash in the water.

i didn't care if people were looking at me.
and if they did,
i would assume it was because
they must love the daisy pattern on my swimsuit.

i never once would have thought
they were thinking poorly of me.
i would have been excited to be seen.
i am trying to find that version of me again.
the girl who hadn't been hurt by the world yet.

Jennae Cecelia

no one in the room is noticing how my hair falls.
or the small grease stain from the pizza
i spilled on my shirt as i hurried to eat lunch.
they aren't noticing the zit i picked on my chin
or the few too many wrinkles in my linen pants.
they aren't questioning why i ordered
both a coffee and a pastry.
they aren't wondering if that is the first thing i ate all day.

no one in the room is noticing these things except me.
but my mind will tell me they are all watching.

DEEP IN MY FEELS

does anyone think of what my body looks like
when someone asks to describe me?
do they say the girl
with the curvy hips and swollen knees?
or do they tell people
i am the girl who writes poetry?
the one who will doodle a picture for you.
talk endlessly about the stars and the moon.
i would like to think
the latter, but
i worry about how i am perceived.

you will act surprised to hear
that she was pretending to be okay.
but how can you be surprised
when you were the one who taught her
to mask her pain?
never asked about her day.
when she did open up just a bit,
you shut it down quick.
a smile on your face so easily permanent.
no one is that happy all the time.
so when you find out she wasn't actually fine,
don't try to look surprised.

DEEP IN MY FEELS

what i am afraid of has changed over the years.
when i was little
it was the storm rolling in.
when i was in middle school
it was wondering how to make friends.
when i was in high school
it was if my anxiety would keep me in bed.
when i was in college
it was the night terrors that followed confronting him.
what i am afraid of has changed
but the feeling of fear is still the same.

i miss the girlhood days
filled with braided hair,
late-night talks,
and truth or dare.
when MASH was played
and our futures seemed far away.
but now we are here.
the adults we once were eager to meet.
except we didn't account for the bills
and pills for anxiety relief.
i wish i could go back to
late nights in my friend's room.
when the possibilities were fun to talk about
because we didn't know all
we would live through.

i remember praying for the pain to go away.
i needed someone to blame.
so it was god or whatever higher power there is.
i wanted to know why this is the life i had to live.
one where my mind couldn't keep calm if it tried.
anxiety running through my veins
and taking over my mind.
i prayed for it to go away.
i heard nothing in exchange.

i almost went to bed without washing my face,
but i remembered that's when i slip up
and start drifting away.

it's one small task that i start putting off.
so much then follows,
because things that matter stop.

who cares if my face is clean
or if i cooked myself a meal this week?
i'll rot on the couch and watch a show.
tomorrow i'll be more productive.

but we already know
that's not true.
tomorrow will come
and i will be in the same mood.
and it all starts with one small thing
i didn't want to do.

he thought it was okay to yell and scream.
to talk down to me.
have no control over
what was coming out of his mouth,
the profanities he would shout.
and i became numb to it all.
i learned to disassociate
while still looking at him like i was listening.

i will say this,
what i thought mattered actually didn't.
opinions i yearned to hear
are no longer around.
i changed myself to fit in
and yet here i am without those friends.
so now i am left as a stranger
to even myself.

who am i when i am not trying to be
who everyone else would like to see?

DEEP IN MY FEELS

he said i was pretty,
but i know that is a lie.
sitting down next to him
i am wondering if he is noticing
my thick thighs.
does he pretend not to care,
or does he really not see them there?
i want to believe he thinks i am beautiful,
but it is hard to do
when i see myself as a giant balloon.

as a child i didn't understand.
but now as an adult i do.

i know that you love me.
i know that you miss me.
i know that is all true
even though it's hard for you to say.
i know showing emotions isn't easy for you.

the good or the bad.
you are even-keeled.
it is all you have ever known.

but i am breaking the cycle
of keeping my emotions tucked away
for only me to face.

i know that might not be easy for you to hear.
i know that you might not understand.
because you still keep all your emotions in.

FEELING HOPEFUL

DEEP IN MY FEELS

i wake up for the first time in days
with that come-back-to-life feeling you get
when the fog clears and you can think again.

i made my bed instead of leaving it a mess.
i called the people waiting for my response.
even chatted longer than was needed.
because i feel cheerful again.

a feeling that was dormant
now active.
happy-go-lucky me is back.

and no one knows the dark days i faced
because i am good at hiding away.
only to emerge when i can
put a smile on my face.

Jennae Cecelia

i thought it could never be true.
that the hurt would slowly fade
like a healing bruise.
surely this pain in my head
from worry and dread
would never go away.
but it did.
and now sometimes
it is hard to even remember
why it kept me up late
or made me say no to going new places.

DEEP IN MY FEELS

i met my younger self for coffee at 10:15.
she was late.
i was early.
i wore my dark brown hair in a slicked-back bun.
her hair was faded red and in her face.
i had dark blue jeans on.
she wore sweatpants with a few stains.

she lets out a sigh and has a good cry.
i tell her to release her feelings one at a time.
the scars on her have now faded on me quite a bit.
i want to tell her it won't always be like this.
but i don't.
she doesn't need to hear
that things will be better.
she just wants a hug and reassurance of her feelings
during this uncertain season ahead of her.

we leave the aroma of coffee beans and baked goods.
i walk her home to our old neighborhood.
we won't meet again for fifteen more years.
but each day she thinks of the woman
who acknowledged her tears.

Jennae Cecelia

i am sorry i stopped being
the me you once knew.
i left prematurely.
i had to.
the waves came crashing in.
the noise was so loud i had to descend.
that version you knew now lost at sea.
don't send a diving team
to find that version of me.
i put her to rest.
it was for the best.

i am sorry i stopped being
the me you once knew.
but this version is better,
i promise you.

DEEP IN MY FEELS

i love that new beginnings have no expiration date.
maybe today is the day for beautiful change.
the color will come back to your face.
you won't always carry this weight.

Jennae Cecelia

i hope we can always meet for breakfast
before our busy day.
sit at our kitchen table
from facebook marketplace.
the sunlight hits just perfectly on your face.
we talk about how everything for once
seems to be going our way.
sometimes we won't get to have this moment
and that is okay.
through the good and bad days.
i'll save you a seat always.

i am the weird girl.
i wear outfits that don't really match.
i have frizzy hair.
i snort a bit when i laugh.
i talk about the stars far too much.
i think too deeply about finding true love.
i am the weird girl.
but that is okay.
i have learned to love myself this way.

i started to believe in love again.
i didn't dread the weddings with a plus-one invitation.
i was okay with being the bridesmaid.
it wasn't my turn yet.
i would smile as the couples danced together.
and no longer be jealous of their closeness.
i started to believe in love again
the moment i met you.

one day i will stop buying clothes that aren't my size
for me to say, *one day i will fit into them.*
they are now gathering dust in my closet.
a reminder for me to get it together.
but it wasn't about the clothes or my size.
i would never be truly happy
until i took care of my mind.

Jennae Cecelia

what do i do with my loud child?

you mean the one who
dances,
sings,
and questions everything.
the first to raise their hand to read in class.
not afraid to let out their laugh.

the one who makes jokes to their family over dinner
and burps louder than they should have
while chugging a glass of coke.
making bubbles with their chocolate milk at breakfast
as they wait for their eggos.

love that loud child.
the world will be quick
to make them feel like they have to be silent.

DEEP IN MY FEELS

for a long time i didn't think that i deserved love.
that my hand would never be gently met.
a kiss placed upon my neck.
that i would live a lonely life.
no one wanting to be by my side.
but now i know that isn't true.
i just chased the kind of love that isn't love,
but rather the kind that disguises itself to get to you.

the pretty girl in high school
is still the pretty girl twelve years later.
except now you don't look at her
with jealousy-laced eyes.
you found a love for yourself
you never could have at fifteen.

maybe what you are mistaking for boredom
is actually your nervous system calm for the first time.
you are used to your heart beating fast.
worrying about getting to the next task.
you have been addicted to the feeling of go, go, go.
your body has finally made calmness your new home.
how beautiful.

Jennae Cecelia

i started to get more excited about
the tomatoes growing in my garden
far more than i did with going to parties
where people don't pull weeds,
they smoke it.
i started to get more excited about
making my own kombucha
far more than i did about downing boxed white wine.
i started to get more excited about
waking up early enough to meet the sunrise
far more than i did falling asleep just before it comes up.
eighteen-year-old me would probably think i am boring,
but i am just happy we made it to see
that this is the person we have become.

there are few things in life
i truly need.
but the sunrise,
the breeze,
and you beside me
are at the top of my list,
if i can be greedy.

friendships can bloom in any season of life.
don't give up hope on finding
the supportive and caring people
you want by your side.
it is okay if you didn't meet years ago.
sometimes the best of friends
are the ones you are just getting to know.

DEEP IN MY FEELS

i think you were afraid
that the butterflies in your stomach would die.
that you wouldn't get excited again
when you see them for the rest of your life.
the novelty would wear off.
but i want to let you know
that couldn't be further from the truth.
they will forever mean everything to you.

i met someone.
he leaves the lights on for me when i am out late.
he has the coffee pot ready to brew in the morning.
he sets out reminders for appointments i have that day.
he hangs my art on the walls in his office.
he does the dishes after dinner and wipes the counters clean.
he asks to hear more stories about what i did in high school
or as a kid.
he fixes things around the house and never shouts.
i met someone and i am certain for the first time ever
that it will work out.

when you are in your twenties,
everyone is telling you that you don't have much time.
hurry up and get married.
hurry up and have kids.
hurry up and get out of debt.
time is ticking.
do you know you only have a few more minutes?

you better have everything crossed off
the societal milestone list
or you are a lost cause.
but i think this is when you are
just starting to bloom.
you make better decisions.
clarity in your mind has entered the room.
time may be ticking,
but life is just getting started for you.

i know you are in a hurry
to what you think is the next best thing.
i will be there soon.
life is just moving so quickly.
i want to take in this view.

DEEP IN MY FEELS

i used to count calories,
but now i order whole-milk lattes
and eat bacon with my pancakes
instead of skipping breakfast altogether.
i don't have to tell my mom
no thanks
when she makes her homemade lasagna and apple pie.
i have seconds of both and don't blink an eye.
and i smile inside because i am finally at peace.
it's no longer war within my body.

it wasn't perfect.
life, that is.
it was hands-in-the-dirt messy at times.
but beautiful things found a way to bloom
in the spots i thought were empty in my life.

DEEP IN MY FEELS

he was summer sun
and winter cold.
the perfect timing.
not too early.
not too late.
he was here right when
i needed him to be.

Jennae Cecelia

the smell after it rained,
the way the birds sang,
the first summer day,
and a meal with friends as laughter is exchanged.
all things that brought me back to life.

DEEP IN MY FEELS

i knew you were the one when you
let me have the pickle that came with your sub
because you knew how much i loved them.

i knew you were the one when you
asked the waitress three times if they made sure
there were no peanuts in the dessert i picked out.
and even then, i could tell you were a little panicked
watching me eat it.

i knew you were the one when you
would listen intently about my thoughts on sleep
and how weird it is that we turn ourselves off
and go somewhere else each night.

it was the small things that were actually big things
that helped me know you were the one.

Jennae Cecelia

i used to hate the waiting season.
but now i realize it is stretching me
to get me to a place that is beyond
what i could have dreamed.

DEEP IN MY FEELS

i let my dog out in the morning
as i make hot water for my lemon tea and ice roll my face.
she is running circles in the yard.
i smile in the doorway as the steam rolls off my mug.
she has everything she needs.

but it wasn't always this way.
for her or for me.
she comes with her own trauma from being displaced.
left out in the rain.
in the car she still shakes.
i try to tell her it is going to be okay.
but i have anxiety, too, so i know you can say that,
but that doesn't make it true.
she and i have a lot in common in that way.

with me she is home.
secure and safe.
and as she runs up to give me a kiss,
i say, *i hope everyone finds that person for themselves someday.*

Jennae Cecelia

you have to date yourself.
eat good food at a table set just for you.
meet the sunrise for a golden kiss.
turn pages in a new book.
pick out a colorful outfit as you thrift.
stretch your body with the wind.
pick wildflowers as you stroll.
you have to date yourself
because then you will realize
you can do things on your own.

DEEP IN MY FEELS

my husband braids my hair for me.
he never once complains.
he brushes it gently
away from my face.
he doesn't tell me it is too tangly.
he never says i should cut it short
if i can't keep it neat.
my husband braiding my hair
heals the inner child in me.

Jennae Cecelia

i have spent so much of my life
thinking about meeting the sunrise
long before she is ready.
dwelling on a past that has
been put to rest
for quite some time.
i wonder when the present and i will meet
and truly enjoy the time we have together.
where we talk about the now
and not what has left or is to come.
where we embrace what is
right here in front of us.

DEEP IN MY FEELS

i spent the morning with clothes on my floor
and tears in my eyes,
because nothing i was putting on my body
i liked.

i finally settled on a pink sweater and some jeans.
it didn't quite feel like me.
but i moved on with my day
and told myself tomorrow we get back on track
and lose some weight.

as i made my way down the sidewalk
i crossed paths with a little girl drawing with chalk.
she smiled big at me and said,
i love your sweater. you look so pretty in it.

that day she healed a piece of me.
and i think i learned to fall in love with myself again.

he is everything i needed,
but so am i.
that is the partnership
i have always wanted to find.
one where we both shine.
never needing to dim our lights.

DEEP IN MY FEELS

i wish i had met you earlier.
i needed someone like you at the end of my days.
in the back of my mind maybe i knew you were coming.
maybe i heard the tiptoes of your arrival
long before you came knocking at my door.
maybe that is what i held on to hope for.

Jennae Cecelia

a man will come and love me deeply.
he won't ask for me to change who i am.
he will embrace all of my stories and
the scars that lie about my body.
he will have empathy for me
but view me as nothing less than strong.
i won't have to hide parts of me that i have been afraid
for the spotlight to shine on.
he has seen and heard it all.
and he is here for me regardless.

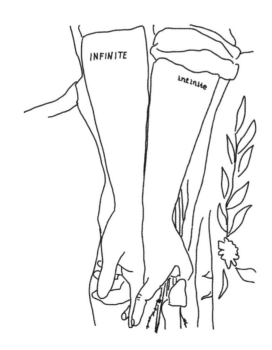

DEEP IN MY FEELS

one day i will be able to tell the version of me
who starts each morning with a cup of coffee,
shaky hands,
and a side of tears
that the skies stopped being scary gray
and the sun is now here.

i know she will cry with joy
right along with me.
she will hum as she waits for her coffee,
take a few deep breaths,
and let her mind go clear.
it is all we ever wanted.
for our story to no longer be one of only fear.

have you heard about . . .
no, i haven't.
for once i am focusing on myself.
i am done ignoring my own life because i want to be someone else.

i am falling in love with painting again.
writing letters to my friends.
taking photos with my digital camera.
meeting the fresh air for some deep breaths.

so no, i haven't heard about the latest gossip,
what style is trending,
or what i just have to buy.
i am truly taking care of myself
for the first time.

i think of the little girl i once was
as i stare in the mirror and pick apart every inch of me.
what would she think of me now?
would she smile and be proud?
i think the little girl i once was would tell me this,
remember how much we used to love how our hair was blown about?
we carelessly would laugh and shout.
we thought the scabs on our knees were fascinating.
we wore outfits that didn't match.
rainboots and a winter hat. and we didn't care.
remember how beautiful that felt?
to love yourself so much that you never even thought twice
to look at your reflection with doubt.

i think there are past versions of me
that get together for coffee.
they talk about who i used to be
and how i overcame
all that was thrown at me.
they don't gossip,
talk badly,
or bring up all of my mistakes.
they meet for coffee
and cheer me on every single day.

DEEP IN MY FEELS

i have waited a long time
to feel clarity in my mind.
the breath in my body
feels like it is happening for the first time.
the color in my skin has started to come back.
people are telling me that i am glowing
but i am the only one who knows why.
i am no longer a shell of myself,
i am fully alive.

ABOUT THE AUTHOR

Photo Credit: Mo Speer Photography

Jennae Cecelia is a bestselling author and poet, recognized for her books *The Sun Will Rise and So Will We* and *Healing for No One but Me*. Starting in 2016, she self-published her debut book—*Bright Mind Empty Souls*—which became a #1 bestseller on Amazon. Her mission is to write words that comfort and resonate deeply with her audience. Jennae spends her time creating custom poetry for readers, turning her poems into illustrated pieces, and teaching other authors how to share their writing with the world.

You can follow @JennaeCecelia on all social media for announcements and new work.